ABANDONED
NORTHERN
OHIO

D1519157

JEFFREY STROUP

AMERICA
THROUGH TIME®
ADDING COLOR TO AMERICAN HISTORY

For my sisters, Caiti and Emily

America Through Time is an imprint of Fonthill Media LLC
www.through-time.com
office@through-time.com

Published by Arcadia Publishing by arrangement with Fonthill Media LLC
For all general information, please contact Arcadia Publishing:
Telephone: 843-853-2070
Fax: 843-853-0044
E-mail: sales@arcadiapublishing.com
For customer service and orders:
Toll-Free 1-888-313-2665

www.arcadiapublishing.com

First published 2020

Copyright © Jeffrey Stroup 2020

ISBN 978-1-63499-213-8

Typeset in Trade Gothic
Printed and bound in England

CONTENTS

ABOUT THE AUTHOR

JEFFREY STROUP first fell in love with photography after finding a camera on the side of the road as a teenager. Years later he discovered urban exploration, the hobby of exploring abandoned places or any other off-limits areas. He has now been exploring and photographing abandoned locations for over fifteen years. His passion for photography and love of history has led him to explore abandoned buildings throughout the country. His work has been featured on Live on Lakeside, *Scene Magazine*, and The Weather Channel. He currently lives in the Tremont neighborhood of Cleveland with his wife, Kaylah.

INTRODUCTION

Northern Ohio is a juxtaposition of rural farmland, industrious Rust Belt cities, and urban sprawl. This, along with the ebbs and flows of a drastically shifting population, has led to an assortment of abandoned structures, all with their own stories to tell. From an abandoned greenhouse to hospitals, schools, factories, and even an amusement park, Northern Ohio has no shortage of forgotten monuments to the past.

After roughly fifteen years of exploring abandoned places, I have amassed countless stories and unforgettable experiences. From getting hopelessly lost in an old asylum, to stumbling upon a human torso in a dark stairwell (it turned out to be a mannequin, but that first glimpse was a terrifying moment). In my first book, *Abandoned Cleveland*, I shared photos from the many vacant structures throughout Cleveland; however, so many incredible abandoned buildings reside outside of the city. There is nothing like waking up before dawn, packing up your camera gear, and making a two-hour drive to an unfamiliar building to capture it in the beautiful early morning light, and be headed home, coffee in hand, before most people have gotten out of bed.

My aim has always been preservation. I want to preserve these places before they are inevitably reduced to dust by either the elements and time, or a demolition crew. The other threat facing these structures are humans with no respect. While abandoned buildings have long been an attractive canvas for graffiti artists, they are also subject to metal thieves, arsonists, and the immature who simply want to destroy, or perhaps even worse yet, cover every surface with their social media handles in a desperate plea for attention. Therefore, certain vulnerable locations within this book are not called by name, and locations and other key details have been left out. My goal is to educate and entertain, not to contribute to further decline and decay.

1

BLACKBURN PLAT

September 19, 1977, might have been uneventful to most of the world; however, to those in Youngstown and the surrounding Mahoning Valley area, it is known as Black Monday. On that overcast day with a slight rain falling, 4,100 people showed up to work only to learn that they no longer had jobs. Youngstown Sheet and Tube had closed its Campbell Works plant. Within five years, the area saw a total of 50,000 jobs disappear. It was the birth of the Rust Belt.

In a city which, at the time, was known for its record high homeownership, above-average wages, and almost non-existent unemployment, the closing of the Campbell Works began a drastic change in momentum. This and the subsequent decline of related steel-dependent industries saw the city of 150,000 dwindle to its current population of less than 65,000. The neighborhood known as Blackburn Plat was especially ravaged by this population decline.

The neighborhood was built by Youngstown Sheet and Tube beginning in 1918 as a response to a steelworker strike that resulted in a riot nearly destroying East Youngstown. The prefabricated concrete design of the housing project was the first of its kind. A two-story house, complete with four rooms and a basement, could be built by a team of five people in just one ten-hour workday. These houses, with amenities including indoor plumbing and electricity, were practically luxurious to the workers they were built for.

In 1940, Youngstown Sheet and Tube sold Blackburn Plat and shortly after Black Monday, the once picturesque housing development quickly fell into despair and eventual abandonment. Today many of the homes sit empty, some even falling victim to arson, but there is hope on the horizon. In 2013, the non-profit group Iron Soup Historical Preservation started purchasing and rehabilitating some of the homes as housing for veterans.

A covered alleyway between two buildings in the workers' housing complex. (2019)

A variety of colors both on the building and in the early morning sky. (2019)

Looking into the kitchen and out the backdoor from inside one of the small living rooms. (2019)

A broken toilet is the only remaining fixture in this bathroom. (2019)

The basement entryway where workers, filthy after a long day of work, could shower and change clothes before entering the rest of the house. (2019)

An upstairs bedroom. Nothing left but peeling paint. (2019)

Looking out through a broken window at some of the other buildings. (2019)

Stuffed animals sitting in a kitchen cupboard. (2019)

The ruins of a kitchen. (2019)

Dramatic paint peel in the bedroom. (2019)

Another kitchen. Although the buildings were prefabricated, the layouts varied unit to unit and building to building. (2019)

More stuffed animals. This time in a bedroom that was littered with other children's toys. A reminder that the collapse of Youngstown's steel industry was felt not only by the factory workers but their families as well. (2019)

Instead of the buildings being painted all the same color, the exterior of each unit was unique. (2019)

A closer view of the alley between the buildings. (2019)

2

MEDUSA CEMENT

On the shore of Lake Erie sits an imposing concrete structure. These silos are all that is left of a massive cement plant. This was the first plant built by Medusa Cement. Medusa started as Sandusky Portland Cement Company in 1892 and was later renamed Medusa Portland Cement Co. In 1913, cement from this plant was even sent to London to be used at Buckingham Palace. Medusa eventually expanded to eight facilities across five different states. However, in 1960, this original plant was closed.

For most people, the quick glimpse of the silos peeking out from above the tree line as they drive down Route 2 is all they will ever see of the old plant. Outside of the occasional trespasser, or a freight train rolling past on the tracks just to the east, this plant is largely removed from the modern world. On one side is the lake and on the other, woods that continue to grow taller and thicker, offering the old building privacy in its retirement.

Exploring silos such as these is far different from exploring just about any other abandoned building. There is not much to actually explore. On my first visit, I never even made it up and into the rooms at the top of the building. To be honest, I had no idea how much was up there. Instead, I spent my time walking around the outside trying to capture just how big and intimidating the place was. On a return visit, determined to be more thorough in my documentation, I made the somewhat sketchy climb to the upper reaches of the silos. I was rewarded with not just an incredible view, but also large rooms and plenty of rusty machinery.

Despite its commanding size and long history, Medusa sits alone, mostly forgotten, and maybe that's the way it should be. Far away from developers who only see dollar signs, out of reach of disrespectful kids bent on destruction, and out of sight of the overly concerned who see every vacant structure as nothing more than hideous blight that needs to come down.

The proud silos of Medusa Cement. (2016)

Trees sprout up between buildings. (2016)

Another view of the great structure. (2016)

The humidity and bugs made my most recent visit a bit unpleasant. (2019)

After climbing a makeshift web of ropes and a few flights of rusty stairs, you come to a room with hoppers and conveyor belts. (2019)

Looking out over the trees from a walkway connecting the two giant silo structures. (2019)

A large room on top of the silos. (2019)

One of the bridges between the buildings. (2019)

Another view from between the silo buildings. (2019)

A rusted drum, its contents unknown. (2019)

The roof offers a fantastic view of the lake and surrounding area. (2019)

Stairwell leading down to where two curved walls of the silos meet. (2019)

A final look at what remains of the huge cement plant. (2019)

3

CHIPPEWA LAKE AMUSEMENT PARK

Chippewa Lake Amusement Park has been a long-standing staple in the urban exploration community. Decades of neglect have left this once bustling park to slowly succumb to nature as well as repeated arson. The remaining rides and buildings are being strangled by vines and bulldozed by the trees growing up around them. The mix of rust and charred skeletons of buildings sits in stark contrast to the rural lakeside landscape.

The park dates all the way back to 1875. It began as Andrew's Pleasure Grounds, and its first roller coaster had to be manually pushed up the track. In 1898, Mac Beach bought the park. His son, Parker, eventually purchased the park and managed it along with his wife, Janet, and is reportedly buried in an unmarked grave somewhere on the property.

The amusement park operated for over 100 years, but after the 1978 season, the decision was made to cease operations. In 2008, development plans were proposed, some of the land cleared, and rides removed. It appeared to be the end of the beloved park. However, in 2012, after some legal trouble, the development plans were scrapped, and the few remaining remnants of the park were once again left to be consumed by nature.

I don't recall exactly when I first visited Chippewa Lake, but I remember being surprised at just how overgrown the place was. It was like going on a nature walk, and every so often you would round a bend in the trail and see a building or ride almost hidden by trees and brush. Braving poison ivy and mosquito bites I did my best to document all remaining aspects of the park. During that first visit, I ran into multiple other people hiking through the property. Even an entire family was out for a stroll, the kids of whom were most likely receiving a fascinating first-hand account of the park from their grandmother. It was nice to see that although the rides have long since slowed to a stop, the park was still being very much enjoyed.

Concession stand "A," which was converted to a restaurant called The Original Hamburger Factory shortly before the park's closure. (2009)

According to some sources, this building was the old bathhouse. However, looking at maps of the park, it seems more likely to be an administration building, with the bathhouse being located further north at the edge of the park. (2009)

The Tumble Bug: one of the most popular rides at the park. (2009)

Another view of the Tumble Bug as trees and plants grow up around it. (2009)

Above left: A paddlewheel boat known as *The Tom Sawyer*. In 2017, the boat was removed from the park and shipped to Tennessee to be restored. (2009)

Above right: Trees growing through the Big Dipper. (2009)

Another view of the concession building. (2009)

The iconic Ferris Wheel, rusted and covered in vines. (2014)

In 2009, much of the land was cleared of trees
to make way for the development that never
happened. Just five years later, nature had
already reclaimed the park. (2014)

Many of the buildings were unrecognizable, and at this point, I'm not aware of any that are still standing other than the ticket booths. (2014)

Ticket booths at the front gate. (2014)

4

AUDUBON MIDDLE SCHOOL

January in Cleveland sees an average of nearly 19 inches of snow. Despite this, I find myself exploring more this time of year than any other time. January of 2019 was no exception. After a brutal snowstorm, and while most people were wisely staying indoors and off the roads, I, along with my wife Kaylah and our friend Jake, made an early morning trip across the city to explore the abandoned Audubon Middle School.

One of the first abandoned buildings that I ever explored was an abandoned school. I don't recall how old the building was, but I remember thinking it must be fairly old based on how different the architecture was compared to the schools that I had attended growing up. The architecture of these older schools is so grand in comparison to more modern schools, which seem to put less thought into appearance, choosing to focus more on function and cost. One of the area's most well-known architects of these beautiful old schools was Walter McCornack. McCornack designed dozens of schools in the Cleveland area, including Audubon.

Audubon was built in 1922 with Gothic Revival elements and beautiful vaulted ceilings in its main hallway. Since its closing in 2010, Audubon's windows have remained nearly entirely boarded up, with only a handful uncovered here and there. Because of this, the interior is shrouded in near-total darkness in most areas of the building. Trying to explore and photograph such a dark building can be challenging. There is also an air of creepiness when all that you can see is what is illuminated with your flashlight beam. With such a limited view of the unfamiliar world around you, it is easy to be taken by surprise—like when you walk into a classroom to find a ghostly white figure in the center of the room. In such darkness, you can't immediately recognize the figure for what it actually is—a perfect pile of freshly fallen snow blown in from a small hole in the ceiling.

The main hallway. (2019)

A tower of snow in the middle of a classroom. (2019)

Paint peeling off the lockers and ceiling makes for a loud crunching sound as you walk through the empty school. (2019)

One of only a few classrooms with light coming in. (2019)

A hallway on the top floor of the building. You can see snow on the ground that had been blown in from an open window, through a classroom, and into the hallway—a testament to the storm the night before. (2019)

A classroom with a few remaining desks. (2019)

The cafeteria with windows looking out into a courtyard. (2019)

One of two gymnasiums in the school. (2019)

The auditorium was incredibly difficult to photograph with such limited light. (2019)

Another photo of the auditorium. (2019)

Soft, blue light illuminates chairs, some still placed neatly on tables as if waiting for a janitor to come sweep the floors. (2019)

5

MASONIC TEMPLE

One of the many elements of exploring an abandoned building is that it feels as if you have been gifted a secret. Stepping outside after having spent a couple of hours exploring every inch of a building that most will never step foot in, especially now that it has been boarded up, you're left with a sense of pride. You have seen and experienced what most people will not. The building and what it holds is now yours. Others might see photos, but they don't have what you have.

While attempting to photograph an abandoned church, only to find an empty lot with freshly planted grass, my friend Jake and I drove off disappointed that we had obviously missed out on our planned location. We didn't get far before Jake pointed out what at the time appeared to be an older office building with a handful of broken windows. I had seen the building before but disregarded it. I had failed to notice the fine details in its architecture, most notably the ornate arched entryway, with a beautifully carved compass and square symbol over the door. This was no run-of-the-mill office building—this was a masonic temple.

Most buildings don't hold any actual secrets; however, masonic temples are an exception. Freemasonry is a fraternity of secrets and their temples and lodges are at the heart of their secrecy. Being able to freely walk around one of these magnificent structures is truly a privilege. Whatever books, ceremonial items, or detailed plans of world domination once housed here were long gone by the time I visited; however, I still walked away with a sense that, just like the Freemasons who regularly met there, I was now privy to some secret knowledge.

I know just enough about freemasonry to know that there would be at least one auditorium. (2019)

This auditorium was very different from the ones I had seen in the Masonic Temple in Cleveland. (2019)

Lockers, all of which were empty, unfortunately. (2019)

Throughout the building, I would occasionally hear noises that always appeared to come from a couple of rooms away. Despite spending over an hour here and walking through the building twice, I was unable to locate the source of any of the noises. (2019)

A second auditorium or lodge room. There was most likely a third one as well, but due to a partially flooded, pitch-black basement, I was unable to find it. (2019)

Seats line the walls. (2019)

Signs that someone was once living here. This was the top floor of the building which means that either a squatter drug this strange assortment of furniture up several narrow flights of stairs or it was already here. Neither scenario makes much sense. Also, please note the full bottle of ranch dressing. (2019)

There was a surprising lack of graffiti and vandalism, other than these broken glass elevator doors. (2019)

What's left of the kitchen. (2019)

These yellow columns looked like pencils. (2019)

I was surprised to see so much color here. (2019)

Another view of the main auditorium. (2019)

6

THE GREENHOUSE

Some of the abandoned buildings that I have explored hold fantastic history, while others are accompanied by wild stories and personal experiences. Others aren't anything special or exciting, just unoccupied structures. The greenhouse doesn't fall into any of these categories. It is one of the most unique places that I have been. In a few short years, I had made several trips to photograph the building. However, when it comes to articulating my thoughts on this beautiful place, I'm left speechless.

Seeing the greenhouse for the first time, I was worried that we would have a hard time exploring the place. From the outside, it looked like a dense forest with a smokestack sticking out from above the trees. I immediately envisioned having to slash a path through the building with a machete. Upon entering, I was surprised to see that the inside was relatively wide open, aside from the occasional tree and small vines that wrapped around rusted pipes and support beams. Walking through the building was, as you might expect, peaceful and meditative. It felt much like any other walk through nature.

Most abandoned buildings offer a sense of adventure—a feeling that you're not welcome. The sense that you are somewhere that you shouldn't be, which obviously you shouldn't be. The greenhouse never prompted those feelings. Instead, it felt welcoming. It felt normal. Despite its uniqueness and beauty, I might go as far as to say that it felt bland. Bland in an emotional sense at least.

Even after four or five visits to the greenhouse, I don't feel as though I ever fully captured it. Nor can I put into words the magic and beauty of the place. It is simply one of those places that can only be experienced first-hand. While it may not elicit strong emotions or be especially exciting to explore, the greenhouse will probably always be one of my favorite locations, even now that it's gone.

Rest in pieces, greenhouse.

Nature engulfing the old greenhouse. (2015)

Once inside, you were able to make out more of the structure. (2015)

A car sitting in the greenhouse with vines weaving their way in and around it. (2015)

The main path through the center of the greenhouse. (2015)

An old cart lays rusting on the ground. (2015)

A pile of terracotta pots with thick vines draped over them. (2015)

Exploring the greenhouse was unlike anything else. At times it was difficult to tell whether you were inside or outside. (2015)

Many of the glass panels have broken. (2015)

Sections of the greenhouse are incredibly thick with vines. (2015)

Tree branches breaking free of the confines of the greenhouse. (2015)

Stacks of terracotta pipe. (2015)

7

THE RUBBER BOWL

The Rubber Bowl was designed by Osborn Engineering Company and completed in 1940 with a seating capacity of over 35,000. For sixty-eight years, the University of Akron's football team, the Akron Zips, called the stadium home. It also served as a concert venue for acts such as The Rolling Stones, The Grateful Dead, Metallica, Aretha Franklin, Bob Dylan, and many others. The final Zips football game at the stadium was played on November 13, 2008. There was a special ceremony after the game to honor the old stadium.

Not long after the university had moved their games to a new stadium, a marketing company purchased the Rubber Bowl with plans to update the press box, locker rooms, and concession areas, along with installing new scoreboards and seating. There was even talk of building a dome over it. However, after five years, these plans never came to fruition, and the county foreclosed on the aging stadium. A few months later, on September 22, 2017, it was announced that the stadium would be demolished.

In the time between that final football game and its eventual foreclosure, the Rubber Bowl had deteriorated significantly. Large sections of seating had been ripped up, the locker rooms and concession areas stripped down to bare concrete, and portions of the AstroPlay field that had been installed in 2003 were ripped up and removed. Graffiti littered the walls, and the restrooms had been reduced to nothing more than scattered and broken porcelain.

On my first visit, I was struck by the size of the place. I had been to sporting events in stadiums much larger than this one, but without thousands of other people filling the space it felt so much bigger. I remember standing at the top row of seats, staring out into the massive structure as if it was the Grand Canyon. After about an hour of taking photos and exploring, I noticed a couple college-age guys walk in. I assumed they were there just to look around, but once they made their way down to the field, I realized they had brought a football with them and had come to the abandoned stadium to play catch. I have never been into sports, but I stopped to watch them for a few minutes and couldn't help but wonder if this was their way of living out some childhood football dream.

Looking out over the stadium. (2016)

The stadium was built into the side of a hill, so much so that even from the top row of bleachers you would still have to walk uphill to exit the stadium at George Washington Blvd. (2016)

Numbers stenciled along the bleachers. (2016)

The stairs leading up to the press box were long gone, which meant that you had to climb to get up there. (2016)

Ramp leading into the interior of the stadium. (2016)

Once inside, you could see the massive pillars of concrete that supported the seating above. (2016)

Much of the interior was unrecognizable. I know that at one time there would have been locker rooms, concessions, offices, and maintenance areas. However, by the time I explored it, it was difficult to tell what was what. (2016)

Smashed toilets in one of the restrooms. (2016)

If you look closely, you can see the two people who had come to the stadium to play catch. (2016)

Inside of a cramped tunnel that ran between the bleachers and the field. (2016)

Sections of seating that had been torn up. (2016)

8

LABORATORY & FACTORY

After reluctantly dragging myself out of bed, I grabbed my camera bag and headed south. I was in a race against the quickly rising summer sun. My hope was to reach an abandoned factory building roughly an hour and a half away just as the sun was coming up. When it comes to photography, lighting is everything, and that early morning light is unbeatable. I made a brief detour to pick up a much-needed energy drink and was feeling good as I approached the factory just as the sun was breaching the horizon. That's when I saw the heavy equipment. The dump trucks. The broken building. My reason for waking up at 4:30 in the morning was half demolished.

Defeat swept over me and I began to make my way back to the freeway. I didn't get far though; in fact, I didn't even make it around the block before another abandoned factory building caught my eye. You could tell it was old, but despite its age it appeared to be in excellent condition. It was a large complex of buildings. Actually, at the time it was built it was considered to be one of the largest factories in the state.

I parked my car and went for a walk around the outside of the building. I had left my camera in the car, assuming there was most likely no way into the building. No more than five minutes later I was jogging back to my car to retrieve my camera equipment.

The factory was built in the late 1800s with an additional three-story building completed in 1915. Here, animal medications and ointments were developed and produced. The business flourished and the two men who founded the business used their success to give back to the community. They built a hospital and started a student endowment fund, as well as generously contributed to many other local charities. After a change in ownership, the factory eventually closed its doors in 1990.

The property has changed hands a few times over the last couple of decades, but remains unused and largely ignored. The loss of this great building would be a tragedy whether the surrounding community realizes it or not. My hope is that someone sees potential in this old factory and finds a way to resurrect it from its slowly decaying state, saving not only a beautiful building, but also helping preserve the memory of the former owners' generosity and what they did for their community.

Green plastic over the windows casts entire rooms in an eerie green glow. (2019)

This area of the building was full of sinks and cabinets, so I assume this was the laboratory portion of the building. (2019)

Vines grow up and into the building through one of the few open windows. (2019)

Much of the building was quite dark; however, this section of the building had beautiful lighting. (2019)

In some areas of the building, the floor had very nearly rotted or completely rotted away, making some rooms difficult to get to or inaccessible altogether. (2019)

Another example of severely compromised flooring. I have no doubt that had I taken a couple more steps I would have found myself on the ground of the floor below. (2019)

Since many of the windows were boarded up, the limited light sources made for dramatic lighting. (2019)

From the outside, the building looks strong and stable; however, the inside tells a different story. (2019)

The tallest part of the factory is the silos at the rear of the building. This image was taken in the room on top of the silos. (2019)

A fireplace in a corner office. (2019)

This area of the factory contained quite a few offices. (2019)

The basement and lower levels of the complex, with their haunting green light, were fun to explore and also easy to get lost in. (2019)

A single chair in an otherwise empty room. (2019)

9

REPUBLIC RUBBER

Acres of crumbling brick buildings, piles of debris, and large patches of concrete spill out across the ground as eerie reminders of where buildings once stood. It would be easy to mistake the ruins of this factory complex for some war-torn country or the aftermath of a terrible earthquake. Seeing it the way it is now, it is difficult to imagine 2,300 people working here, manufacturing tires and hoses for the auto and aerospace industries.

Founded as Republic Rubber and built on the site of the American Belting Company in 1902, Republic's tires were sold worldwide. Innovations in tire technology developed by Republic led to early success. In 1914, Republic became one of the first companies in the area to build a recreational facility for its employees that included a cafeteria, showers, and even bowling. For years business thrived; however, that began to change in the 1970s and 1980s. After years of uncertainty, the plant permanently closed in 1989.

For the last three decades, the once bustling 48-acre plant has been left for ruin. By the time I first visited the site in 2012, it was already a well-known and much-visited spot for photographers and urban explorers. Buildings are scattered throughout the site. Between them, trees and plants have grown up among the ruins and on the piles of bricks and debris, the only remains of buildings that haven't survived. Near the center of the complex, a lone smokestack stands tall and proud. Holes that drop into basement levels litter the landscape, ready to swallow up anyone foolish enough not to watch where they walk. Photos don't capture the feeling one has while exploring the property. The cliché post-apocalyptic reference is unavoidable here. You truly get the sense that you have wandered into a world ravaged by some great disaster.

A dark ominous sky seems fitting for this post-apocalyptic wasteland. (2017)

Foundations of buildings long-since demolished. (2017)

Not much remains of the factory as far as furniture, fixtures, tools, and machinery. However, there are a few rooms here and there still containing desks, workbenches, shelves, and other relics. (2017)

Rusted conduit and an old start/stop switch, its purpose lost to time. (2017)

An industrial cathedral. (2017)

Shoes dangle from a cable and blow in the wind. (2017)

The state of decay here seems more akin to a movie set than it does to something that exists in real life. (2017)

Discarded couches and mattresses are a common sight. (2017)

Burnt debris fills a stairwell. (2017)

Interior walls have become exterior walls. (2017)

A rusted doorknob and chipped paint. (2017)

Buildings are scattered throughout the property all in various states of decay. (2017)

Some sort of furnace in the basement of one of the ruined buildings. (2017)

10

CHURCH OF BOOKS

Many buildings lose their original purpose over time. I've seen factories and warehouses converted to apartments, old schools turned into nursing homes, and fire stations reborn as coffee shops, but churches tend to remain churches. These old ornate cathedrals with their vaulted ceilings, bell towers, and cavernous sanctuaries can be difficult to re-purpose without imagination and lots of money.

In the western reaches of the state sits a church originally founded in 1894. Its building was dedicated in 1907, with an addition added in 1922. The beautiful structure sat proudly until 1958, when it fell victim to an arsonist's flame; the sanctuary was destroyed. This was just one of many suspicious fires that swept the city around that time. The congregation never rebuilt, and the building was eventually purchased by a local college who turned it into a library. The roof, which was nearly entirely consumed by the fire, was replaced with a flat roof, and within the nave they constructed the three-story library.

Just fifteen years later the college closed, leaving the library and all the books within to rot away. In the early '90s, a new congregation moved into the building. They didn't do much renovation or construction work. In fact, the library remained almost untouched. Instead, they opted to use an auditorium in the lower level of the building as their meeting place. However, they did not stay long, leaving the building to fall into a depressing state of decay and ruin.

Today, the three-story metal structure that was built to house 52,000 books is quickly rusting away and threatening to collapse under the weight of all those books that were left behind. As a lover of books and architecture, it saddens me on multiple levels to see something so beautiful reach the point of no return.

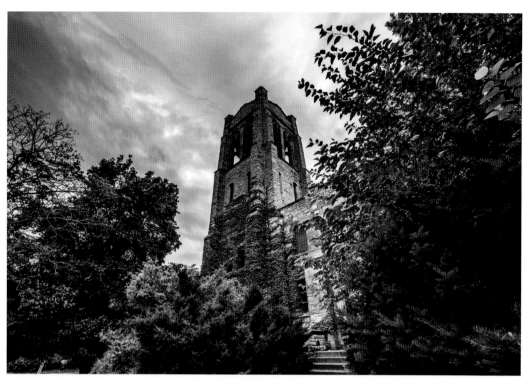

Bushes and trees grow out of control and vines snake their way up the old bell tower. (2019)

You can see on the left where rust has started to eat away at the metal structure containing the library. (2019)

Colorful old desks and scattered papers. (2019)

The second floor of the library still has shelves full of books. (2019)

A close-up of some of the books. (2019)

Toward the front of the church, the floors are soft from years of water damage. (2019)

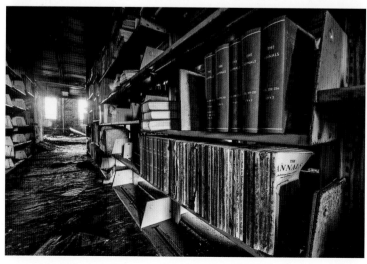

More old books, many of them moldy and waterlogged. (2019)

The church would have been beautiful in its day. (2019)

Stairs lead up to the third floor of the library. (2019)

Another view of the library structure. (2019)

The bell tower with no bell. (2019)

The greens of ferns and moss contrasting with the reds and oranges of rust. (2019)

This basement auditorium was an unexpected surprise. (2019)

Fine detail along the sides of the seats. (2019)

11

ST. JOSEPH RIVERSIDE HOSPITALS

Hospitals, whether active or closed, new or old, are confusing buildings. St. Joseph Riverside Hospital in Warren is no exception. The hospital was founded by Dr. Chester Waller, and in 1924 The Sisters of the Humility of Mary assumed ownership. In 1970, an eastern wing was added, followed by a southern wing in 1980. These large additions, other improvements, and reconfigurations over the years make for a somewhat convoluted layout. It is easy to lose yourself inside the dark and decaying hospital building.

The basement is dark and partially flooded. The first-floor hallways are caked in soggy ceiling tiles that have fallen to the floor. The upper floors are covered in moss and small plants. I have been in older hospital buildings, ones that have been abandoned much longer, but this one is without a doubt in one of the worst conditions I have ever seen. You would be hard-pressed to find a single intact window. Just about anything that can be broken, smashed, or shattered has been. The result of scrappers, and teenage angst and showboating. In December 2018, two separate rooms in the basement of the old building were set on fire.

The hospital closed in 1996 but was partially reused until 2008. It wasn't long after its closure that I first heard about it and began to see photos taken there by fellow explorers. Despite this, and its relatively close proximity, it wasn't until 2017 that I finally made my way there to see it for myself. I was surprised to see just how far gone the building was. I spent a long time inside trying to see every part of the hospital, but navigating the dark maze-like structure wasn't easy. The basement was especially confusing. There was even a passageway behind one of the rooms that became more and more narrow as you walked through it. It was like something out of a funhouse.

I'm not sure how much longer this building will be standing. The city claims that it doesn't have the funds to tear it down. Regardless of how it comes down, its demise is most likely inevitable and fast approaching.

One of the many hallways. (2017)

I'm not sure what this room would have been used for, but it was the only one that I saw with green tiled walls like this. (2017)

Light pours out into an otherwise dark hallway. (2017)

Moss and grass growing on old ceiling panels.
(2017)

I had to duck down to pass through this little arched doorway. I assume it was a playroom for kids. (2017)

Moss and mold overtake an old Styrofoam food container. (2017)

Peeling paint in varying colors ranging from pink to pastel purple and blue. (2017)

An old chair sits in front of a crumbling wall. (2017)

The end of a hallway. The floor was wet and slippery, and you could see footprints in the muck left behind by previous explorers. (2017)

Clockwise from top left:

A dim beam of light illuminates some sort of moldy growth on the wall. (2017)

One of a dozen sets of stairs that we followed while trying to make our way around the building. (2017)

Whatever was used to cover the walls is now peeling off in sheets. (2017)

Two large windows on the ground floor. (2017)

A chair guards the stairs leading up from one of the lower levels of the building. (2017)

12

THE TRAILER PARK

Dozens of abandoned mobile homes, trailers, and tiny cabins litter the lakeside landscape. To one side, crumbling docks stretch out into the water; to the other, freight trains thunder down tracks. At one point this would have been the location of long-awaited summer vacations and weekend getaways. Today it is a wasteland of sad, dilapidated trailers. Many are painted in once bright, almost obnoxious colors, with names ascribed to them such as "The Escape Hutch" and "Serenity." Clearly, this was a summertime haven for its long-gone residents.

One striking feature of this secluded summer getaway is just how much was left. Why would you leave so many of your possessions? Why leave your trailer or mobile home at all? The greatest benefit to owning one of these is that they can be moved to a new location, so why did no one bother to relocate? One can only assume that the closure of the park was unexpected and sudden; that financial restraints left residents no other option than to chalk it up as a loss and walk away. Regardless of the reasoning behind this, the number of toys, books, food, board games, and furniture gives this post-apocalyptic paradise a very real human element. I am always left feeling sad for this place and for the people who once cherished their time here.

The somewhat remote location has helped to keep vandalism to a minimum. Instead, the destruction work has been left to mother nature, and her cruel and unforgiving Lake Erie winters. I have visited here once or twice a year for the last five years. With each visit, the decline is more and more dramatic. The colors of the trailers seem less vibrant. The cabins are succumbing to nature. The remaining furniture is crumbling and broken. Time is running out for this old trailer park.

At first glance, it is difficult to imagine this place ever being a well-manicured piece of summer paradise. (2019)

Year by year, the trailers and cabins are being overtaken by nature. (2019)

A tangle of vines in an old trailer. (2015)

A cramped bathroom in one of the trailers. (2015)

The sun peeks out from behind one of the little wooden cabins. (2015)

The pink trailer is always a favorite. (2015)

Coloring books, toys, stuffed animals, and other children's items are a common sight. Obviously, this was a place for the entire family to enjoy. (2015)

Eveready once had a battery factory in Cleveland. It was located where the Battery Park neighborhood now sits. (2015)

Some of the cabins are entirely empty, while others have furniture, books, and even old food left in them. (2015)

A couch reduced to little more than springs. (2015)

Looking into the bedroom of one of the trailers. (2017)

Even after several trips to the trailer park, I am still finding things that I had missed on previous trips. (2019)

Vines hang down from the ceiling in one of the small cabins. (2019)

Cans of food in a kitchen cabinet. (2019)

Not every location that I explore holds sentimental value, but certain places do end up finding a special place in my heart. This old trailer park is one of them. (2019)

FINAL NOTE

The question that I am most often asked is: Why? Why do I explore and photograph abandoned places? It is a difficult question to answer. While the reasons that I continue to explore are numerous, I cannot nail down the true driving factor that has pulled me into these abandoned buildings again and again. Curiosity. Adventure. Art. History. All of these things motivate me to keep searching out locations; however, the real compelling factor feels more primal. Like there is a part of me that depends on this for survival. A hunger that can only be satisfied with dirt, rust, and decay. Perhaps it is the emptiness, the solitude, the escape from people and crowds. There is no denying my introversion. Whatever the reason may be, it is written into my DNA. There is no escaping it.

When it comes to the urban exploration community, I mostly keep to myself. The age of Instagram has ushered in a new breed of explorer. One that doesn't always subscribe to the same ethos as the older generations, those of us still following in Ninjalicious' footsteps. That doesn't mean that I don't respect and admire the accomplishments of some of these new explorers. I find great comfort in knowing that there are so many others out there finding new places, pushing the limits of exploration, constantly going deeper, and taking the risks that some of us old-timers aren't willing to take. So, thank you to all of you that are out there doing your thing and keeping this hobby alive.

I would also like to thank everyone that has supported and encouraged me over the years. Jake, you've been a die-hard exploring partner. Jeff, thanks for proofreading and editing this mess. My family, I love all of you so much. And of course, my wife, Kaylah—where would I be without your love and support? Without these amazing people in my life encouraging me to keep chasing my passions, I would be lost, and not the fun kind of lost like the time Kaylah and I got lost in an old abandoned asylum. Finally, thank you to everyone reading this. I am so honored that you took the time to look through my book.